WRITTEN BY AMY BEVERIDGE

ILLUSTRATED BY RUSTY FLETCHER

ISBN 0-7847-1723-0

11 10 09 08 07 06 05

Standard
PUBLISHING
Bringing The Word to Life™

Cincinnati, Ohio

Each year we honor people who spoke out for freedom. . . .

And God is honored even more when we speak out for him.

*May the words of my mouth and the thoughts of my heart be pleasing to you, O L*ORD. —Psalm 19:14

Each year we remember people who gave their lives
for freedom. . . .

And God is pleased even more
when we remember him.

Everything in the heavens and on earth is yours, O LORD. —1 Chronicles 29:11

Each year we thank people who
made sacrifices for freedom. . . .

COMMUNITY EVENTS

We Love Our Veterans
Veterans
Day Picnic

And every Sunday we celebrate Jesus who was born to set us free.

For God so loved the world that he gave his only Son. —John 3:16

Yes, all through the year I can celebrate brave people and special days, sacrifices and symbols. . . .

But I can thank God for my country's freedom and for the freedom Jesus gives every day.

The truth will set you free.
—John 8:32